MW01492065

The head
&
the heart

AISHWARYA IYER

BlueRose ONE
Stories Matter
NewDelhi • London

BLUEROSE PUBLISHERS
India | U.K.

Copyright © Aishwarya Iyer 2024

For permissions requests or inquiries regarding this publication,
please contact:

BLUEROSE PUBLISHERS
www.BlueRoseONE.com
info@bluerosepublishers.com
+91 8882 898 898
+4407342408967

ISBN: 978-93-6261-722-4

Cover design: Rishav Rai
Typesetting: Rohit

First Edition: May 2024

Contents

Cave  me in

The shrapnel of my faith in people cut through my skin, and as I bled, I carried my past wounds while moving slowly towards shelter. The old darkness ineluctably came and I had nowhere left to run. So I cocooned in my little cave, bleeding, and confiding in its silence, in the quiet winter with a frightened whisper, as my words rose in the dark. The shadows were dancing on the rocky floor and I saw you, pale in the middle of the night in the flickers of moonlight. I carried a sense of weariness so I let you in my cave. As you shivered, I set my soul on fire, burning it like cedar to keep you warm. You treated our love like fireworks, keeping the sky amused and now that you are warm, you've left me all alone. I tried looking for you when the fog rolled through but I couldn't find you. I waited there, as the winter turned the meadow brown. I am falling down, like it is a holy ground and I'm looking for you again. Let me shiver and die in your arms and someone can spread my ashes next to your grave. I have woken up from a dream only to find that I still haven't woken up. Or maybe, that's all you were.

A stranger in my cave.
Don't ever let go,
(You have to let go).
I can't let go,
(It is time to let go).

The forest *fire*

We were a burning forest, the blackened branches were like detritus in water. With you gone, I was a flaming branch-scattered into a thousand pieces and my heart drifted like the blazing wood which broke and bowed with wishbones hidden in the residue. The forest was stacked with trepidation and the howling beasts heard every patient thought passing by me and every truth that I said about our bond sounding absurd. I was lost in the nightscapes, beaten on the heftily ponderous ground, down in the darkness where none traced me. We were both cut apart in half by the same wood, by hope, like the robin that cuts the dawn. As the fire settled and the wind started to call my name, yours sorrowfully started to fade away. There were death leaves lying on the ground I walked on. I felt my ghost, wrenching, devoid of love to offer, completely lost. I realised we were both trapped in our own fires and now you're a banished memory. Though we lost touch a while ago, someday I'll come to find you, no matter where you might be, hoping that our flame can be reignited never to be doused again.

An everlasting forest fire.

Don't ever let go,

(You have to let go).

I can't let go,

(It is time to let go).

 *bird*

I was a flightless bird, in my rain-inundated tears, fluttering through the inclement thunderstorm, grounded and bleeding. The lightning had maimed my feathers. I was a carpenter building a home for my morbid lover and the crisp air being hyperborean, there was no room for me to breathe. The weight of people's unbridled expectations and my love for them brought me down, too burdensome for me to carry. They said it was minacious. But I flew anyway. Burnt out, obliterated and abused in the storm, there was no light. Yet, I kept ploughing through. The gloominess of the dark clouds was coming. But the sound of the heftily ponderous pitter patter was nothing when weighed to the sound of me whimpering and sobbing. Squalling in the storm, I could only make it alive to my lover if I let go of the nest I carried. I woefully chose to let go of myself to save them. At the brink of my death, I graciously smiled as my lover cooped up in the warm home I had crafted. The wider the storm, the more expeditiously you bereave, and so breathing in, breathing out, I let stillness reside in my inconsolable death. I am now waiting for you on the other side.

Don't ever let go,

(You have to let go).

I can't let go,

(It is time to let go).

Bottled Up

Blind as the night that finds us all, I was enshrouding beneath the stars and satellites, lovestruck and injudicious, lost in the nightscapes down in the darkness where nobody would find my mind for days. I tried folding my worries over and lighting them under your moon but my grief of losing you fell flat and hollow upon billion-blooded stars. I was battering dreams for the feelings I've sold as I sat there, drinking away my pain in the dead of the night on the grass. There was liquor and love but not enough of each one. Carried by the current of the night miles before the surface of dawn, I seemingly poured my heart and drank out a little more than I was allowed. I am not phased by the darkness in your soul because you lit up my life like the fireflies that ignite the night empyrean, making the blue moon sound like no time at all. I kept probing for you as the sleepless night never seemed to culminate and the sun kept slipping through my algid hands. If every penny I owned was all that you stole, I could have sold my heart for a pocket of gold.

Don't ever let go,

(You have to let go).

I can't let go,

(It is time to let go).

The Sailor Moon

I gave credence to you on a night as dark as the crows, like a sailor who trusts the ocean waves. I was helming, marooned on a boat, while the daunting clouds above began to disembogue and the ocean tossed aside the weary. The howling moon had a name in the fires of a silver corpse as I held the atlas, and it told me I could find you there, with our emotions hiding under the blue surface, and the ocean being your mind while I was disoriented in it. I went north, I went south, roving berserk around the world only to come back running to the echoes of your voice through the water body. The gambling ocean appeared bottomless and the waves whispered to me, murmuring, convincing me to plunge. I was stuck between my head and the horizon, wanting to kiss you underwater expeditiously because little obsessions rule us and in a moment it will all wash away. I wanted to know where the world would transcend the water of your mind so I jumped, succumbing to the whispers of the waves. I could feel the shadows cutting me in moiety, robbing me blind, leaving a cold trail of the last descent. You took away my breath and I think a part of me knew I would die, but I'd rather drown than go on without you.

Don't ever let go,

(You have to let go).

I can't let go,

(It is time to let go).

A Train Ride Home

Emaciated, wilted and wasted away to the ground, feeling like I had lost it all. My love had cruised away and the torment of people hurting the child inside of me had started getting heavier and more gruelling. The sun turned ebony and had started to flicker, while the moon was coming around, as I was lured into the train station with a siren song. It was late and tardy but I dragged myself to my own dark night, blind from the stillness, standing there so quietly like the silent sound of an elevator. I was like a wandering child, keeping an arm's length from the tracks so I would not fall, : waiting for someone, hoping they'd ambulate out the exit door of every train that arrived at the station. While the working class was trudging through their days, and parents were boarding night trains rushing back return to their children, I waited in aloneness like the desolate and companionless. I wonder if I should have stayed there that long chasing the light in the locked door of vacuous, estranged trains. Every breath I took was a sempiternity, but the eternal wait wasn't half as painful as letting go of them, so I chose to dwell in my disasters. Holding on to something I shouldn't need, all this delusion in my head was bringing me down to my knees. The midnight trains were as empty as my stomach and as estranged as my soul, and as I patiently waited for them to arrive my body began to depart the world.

The train was empty after all.

Don't ever let go,

(You have to let go).

I can't let go,

(It is time to let go).

Desert Rain

My breath cascaded out over the golden fields of the sandy desert in thirst and my despondency cleared with a spectacle of lenience running down the hope when you made an empty promise to go bring us water. From drylands to high desert walls, the sun came up, and the heat shrivelled up my tears while I bathed in the sand enduring a gruesome heat. I held my tongue dry as we never swayed and I was tearing down doors of time, sojourning for you as your windshield drawings started to fade. I started seeing shadows of you from the corner of my eye in just a lonely impulse of bewitchment. You looked completely different and bought back an empty glass. The bottom felt fathomless, the summer heat was blistering and the edges of the sand seemed to have gotten sharper. Somebody did return. But it wasn't the same person who left. Beneath my feet, I could feel the hole where the revelation nailed. I loved you nevertheless and bounteously gave you the little water we had, as I died of thirst.

There's strength in the blindness, I fear.

Don't ever let go,

(You have to let go).

I can't let go,

(It is time to let go).

A Hailstorm *of Dead Roses*

My bones were frozen in a cold lover's waltz as I was shivering from the chilly wind you perpetuated in anger and hate. I hid under a blanket of dead roses, lost in the fields trading tales of home. Your gaze was my home. The music was warmer than my blood. A deep blue sea of thoughts overhead and a single drop of rain falling from the sky kissed my face. My head was in my hands as I was shaking, wimping and drowning in golden tears like a baby that cries on the doorstep as you left me with empty pictures filled in my mind. You left me to suffer in agony, in a void of muting hope, absence, and pain. Pain that I'd finally seen through the mask that you donned to cover up your shame. Shame that made you feel unworthy. Unworthiness that arose from your sunken and plummet emptiness. Emptiness, because of which you stay surrounded with people, to resolve what your parents had left you with : a void. Void left behind by their invalidation of your emotions when you were a child. How I only wish you could see my love for you ! Cast away your mask, for I would accept you the way you are. Can't you see that your void and emptiness made me feel more complete and alive than I've felt in years?

So alive, my soul is dead without you .

Don't ever let go,

(You have to let go).

I can't let go,

(It is time to let go).

The  Civil War

You disarmed me with your last smile as I sat there by the blood on your shirt, forlorn, gnawing as I ached to hear your voice through the echoes of children wailing in the warfare. I let them stare, I let the wind eavesdrop as the final sound you heard was the mightiest of guns. I saw you scrimmage in the darkness but the murkiness growing inside, and your inner demons were winning the fight. The words I was aching to hear from you poured through my canyon as I was singing our song in the caverns of my limbs. Your soul bled moonlight into the night's embrace as the shadows passed like ghosts across your lifeless body. Your face had begun to fade but my profound love for you still lingers. You left me here to wither in denial, I was falling into my illusions. I did not know how to hold the weight of my soul while letting you go, I burst into tears. I had never met a better fighter than fear, but it had to be me after all. I will carry my love for you on my shoulders, by the train track which will take all the wounded ones homes. You are my real home and as my feet will march on this holy ground, this love will see the army's fall.

Don't ever let go,

(You have to let go).

I can't let go,

(It is time to let go).

The  Cliffhanger

Your flame was whipping against the cold wind I waded through. The darkness had wooden teeth as the full bellied moon watched over me. I threw my love for you into the ocean on that dark night hoping it'd be washed away but as I stayed by the shore my eyes began bleeding. I stood there awake, dreaming, left with all your secrets to defend as I found myself asking if I could reverse time so you'd bring back the person I knew. I wish you could bring back the person I had known in the beginning. Although your heart has a thousand colours, yet they're all shades of grey like the ocean at night, that I was staring at. I remember when you stood there so ravishing, in the frozen wind and blizzard of ice and you let me come into your storm. I got sucked in as I stumbled across your darkness and I let it follow me home. I now felt like I was walking with a stranger who did not even know their name. When I looked into your eyes then, it seemed like you cared. But now I seem to have become incapable of recognising you anymore. I am hanging onto the pedestal I put you on, petrified of letting go of something that isn't even real. But maybe you and I had a flicker of truth. So meet me at our graveyard.

Don't ever let go,

(You have to let go).

I can't let go,

(It is time to let go).

The  Mirror Lake

I stood there gazing into the still waters, much like Narcissus, where my lover's image dances upon the rippling surface. Oh, Mirror Lake, will you not show me the depths of longing that I know? Will you not reveal the truth behind the love I feel? Do you have the dauntlessness to show me reality? I ask of you. In your shimmering depths, I see a love that is not meant to be, and the ripples reveal that it was not my lover, but a facade of what could be. I foolishly surrendered to its enchantment, although aware of the delusion. In your reflection, I found my desire. And oh ! it was an illusion like I've ever seen, an illusion so beautiful, that I jumped in . I undressed and swam until the sun went to sleep . Never earlier had I felt that calm my entire life before. As my fingers and body met the water's skin, I woke up in a shock, realising it was all just a dream. Ah mirror lake, thou hath deceived me with your calm surface. As I swam beneath your glassy veneer, I realised that underneath it lay a love so insincere. But in reality, it's all just a masquerade. With all my regrets, I watched you wash away. Yet I still kept swimming, for I would much rather swim in this phantom love and a mirage so real, than find safety elsewhere.

Don't ever let go,

(You have to let go).

I can't let go,

(It is time to let go).

The Snow Burial

Oh the bitter winds are coming in, and with time as the howling wind was passing, I was gaining patience. I was already missing the summer, but I was born to endure this kind of weather. The wind, she was crying, heavy and cold. She was as frightened as I was, frightened of the days and years to come, coming in heavy in speed yet totally lost. She was spinning around. There is a world that spins around, tears a hole in my heart that couldn't be repaired, it was better to feel this pain than nothing at all but I won't let them run you down. There are some weights you don't have to burden even if you can't seem to lay them down. When I looked at you I felt my head and grip come loose. Hiding from the weight beneath the moon, I stood there freezing in my skin, dying to hear you call my name one more time. As I kept walking and walking, the thought of losing you made my heart stop and I fell there in the snow, slowly freezing to death, but with a smile on my face.

Perhaps because you were my last thought.

Don't ever let go,

(You have to let go).

I can't let go,

(It is time to let go).

The Photograph

The world is not placable in anyone's fears and I had fallen woeful, needing a place to stay so for a moment I wished for everything to be still. Persistently, I kept looking at a photograph of you and me , hanging onto a still memory of your laughter. Your voice had made it impersonate a dream. Your voice was pulling me stumbling through a symphony like an echo in the chambers of my heart. That photograph, a commemorative of where I could find you again, a light that might give up the way. Without you, I am lost. But strangely, the deeper I was looking, the more you kept absquatulating, you kept running away. You left me with a gnawing and lingering soul as I brokenly kept slipping away, from your finger, your mind. This love was fading way too expeditiously. With rattled apparel, bandits on my eyes and shrapnel in my knee, I couldn't walk, although sweating through my heart as I gradually kept travelling through the photograph. I chose to be a lonesome girl and in her hornswoggled mind, we got married and worked out just fine because I knew how to dream. I have grown weary but I can't stop chasing the past. So, my love, please don't fade away !

Don't ever let go,

(You have to let go).

I can't let go,

(It is time to let go).

The Empty *Diner*

As the night capitulated and surrendered the day to hours, I sat there in the corner of the empty diner alone, with my thoughts consuming me more than my gluttony. I was to partake the last morsel of food when the rays of light came upon the aperture of my broken glass plate. I cannot explain why it evoked your memory. As the light on that fissure mirrored a reflection of our happy days of yore, tears brimmed my face. As I gulped down the last bit, I lost the way home to my body, like it did not rapport to me anymore. The plight of my heart, resemblant to that broken plate, only stimulated the endeavour to find you again. Albeit it had been far too long since I let you go, did I hallucinate your presence a moment ago? Through the broken plate, I had caught a glimpse of your velvet glaze and In the quiet depths of my being's core, the moonlight spilled my secrets.

There was no time to trust, there was still no hope to find, something I was holding onto for a while, but all hope was disoriented. Everything I was now was only leading me up until this point. As I left the diner, my stomach and my heart felt emptier than before.

Don't ever let go,

(You have to let go).

I can't let go,

(It is time to let go).

The  Airport

You were impatiently pacing to take a flight that tore into the colourless skies, whilst you could have taken the beautiful road. Little did I know you would never return to this path. Heftily ponderous were my eyes as I ran blind in love, which were inchmeal, burning to cover up the approaching reality that I did not know was yet to come. I gazed modestly at you as you kissed me goodbye through the best morning. My eyes beheld you as you walked through those departure gates. I had a notion of holding the universe in my palms, I remembered the hopes you had brimmed into my heart when I ran short of fortuity. I promised myself that I'd always be there in the needles and cones, and that no door we walked through would ever make me stop profoundly relishing you. I waited and waited for what appeared to be eternity like a faithful dog awaiting its master's return, finally enlivened to have you back home after a long separation. I was perplexed as I watched a new unrecognisable you. The heavy downpour reminded of the air prevailing in the thick dark cloud of the approaching dusk, bidding adieu to the bright sunny day. My heart was heavy and I felt just as cumbersomely hefty as stone. Scuffling and gnawing to maintain whatever little was left, I spotted the bleeding wound you left in my heart. I do not know how long I stood motionless in that parade of rain as you stepped out into the cold. All I knew was the embrace of a perturbing loud silence that pierced through my soul. The pain was sinking in me, as though I was drowning in the rainwater, as if rushing to bloat my lungs. A part of me still lives with a hope that the person I beheld in those departure gates still resides in the one who returned, yet never returned.

Don't ever let go,

(You have to let go).

I can't let go,

(It is time to let go).

The Broken *Clock*

The clock was ticking and as I was wrapped in dissonance, lost in my insignificance, all I could think of was you. My eyes confounded me as I kept looking at the clock, caught up in circles, as I lived in the rearview wishing for an image of you that I thought was true. I've been trying to find answers to questions I cannot answer and as the days turn into nights, the second hand turns. Seasons kept changing and I asked myself "Before the fall, would things have changed? Was I holding onto nothing ? Is this how it felt to hold back to keep it all alive?". Confusion was nothing new, there were many flashbacks, warm nights, and memories that I was leaving behind. I was too sure of the sun, and it all somehow felt like it all fell in one day. It was getting dark and cold, and these nights were getting longer and longer. I kept trying to steal time and I wanted to live that day like it was my last. This old house is now cold and empty. There was a time I called you mine and the things that kept us apart kept me alive. Just like the clock, there is no turning back.

Don't ever let go,

(You have to let go).

I can't let go,

(It is time to let go).

The Art Exhibition

The artist had painted the canvas with regret and rage. As I stood by the painting, so drawn but oblivious and baffled I felt a strange pull and repulsion, both concurrently. The painting seemed to whisper, conveying its fearfulness of change, asking for my forgiveness as it was stringing for all the things it has done to me. The painting had mystically seized my mind and was compelling me to absquatulate and forsake it. But instead of abandoning it, I lowered my defences and clenched it. What is it that lured me to it, I know not. What was I endeavouring to gain? I know not. Was it just a momentary bliss? I waited for nothing since nothing arrived, except a comical inner battle and a constant game. It was eroding me, eroding my sense of pride. I felt like a little child visually examining art for the first time, prophesying for something to escort me to reality. The hum and the rush were never enough, and I was unsure whether or not to buy it. It seemed as though you verbalised with me through your art. I remained perplexed on how I should perceive those emotions, only that I was heartbroken. I fell in love with your art all over again.

I fell in love with you, the artist, all over again.

Don't ever let go,

(You have to let go).

I can't let go,

(It is time to let go).

The Myth of the Arctic Fox

You were as beautiful as the bewitching Teumessian fox, and on that night, I, an arctic fox, could hear the wind whistling your name and the tundra woods sighing to guide me towards you. The worn-out permafrost knew my feet were tired but I told myself that wouldn't stumble, I wouldn't falter, I would still call for you and venture into this rapture of doubt. In the low light on the flat firmament, some want flesh, some want bone but with the benediction of the father's sons and holy ghosts, I decided there was only one way to light up the sky to find you. The ice would melt, the food might grow but my love did not seem to evanesce. I started to run through the sky as expeditiously as I could, used my tail to sweep the snowflakes and brush them against the mountains, which ineluctably caught the moonlight. I summoned the Aurora to converse with you. The Northern Lights made a whistling sound, howling my love for you through the mountains. As the empyrean lit up with the lights, I whimpered my love for you so loudly, that the welkin now had not just Aurora, but also accompanied by Helios and Seline.

The Tree of

life

Lost out among the trees in the forest, I was disoriented much like the trojan Aeneas as my hand scraped the bark and I had bloody knees, with little to no life at all . I was whimpering in pain but I kept scuttling and pounding, blindly following two doves that told me they would lead me to a sacred branch. As they scampered their way through, all of a sudden, I stumbled across an oak tree that marginally resembled the Golden Bough . Its roots dug deep so into the earth, that it was desperately onto its past, and its branches were reaching towards the sky, as it was eagerly reaching for hope. It was swayed by the wind and swayed by desire but buried deep was a quiet seed. In a land so plenary of leaves I was apprehensive that it was marching away from the stream and it would die without leaves. I prayed with my knees on the ground and as I slowly started humming the song that comforts me, the tree opened up and started bringing forth fruits. Using the blood on my knees, I was using it to carve out good memories in the wood. I made a promise to myself that your leaves will stay green, they won't ever wither like my eternal love for you.

A Church Of Gold

My lover's riches are plenteous, just like the prolific love of Christ and on the night of Christmas Eve, I witnessed the beautiful sight of a church of gold where women and children were singing the sounds of hallelujah. While you were entreating for the redemption for all your sins, I sat there praying for you, plenarily in awe, madly in love with you. I asked you to make your wine of my worship, one that of divine peculiar refrain. On this day, my hands did not feel like mine, they were as if they belonged to you. But heaven knows all this dawdling, these times might not last forever after all. My hands were quivering from the cold air of fear, so I wrapped myself up in a blanket of pain, love, and apparitions. An emergent year, a new beginning, suddenly I decided that I no longer wanted to stay warm in people's blanket of crooked lies, I chose to break my dark dealing ties. I determinedly chose to break those undeserving bonds, never to connect again. I fell in love with you but simultaneously fell in love with my light. I loved you, and at the same time I was drawn immensely by the light. Why did I have to encompass my love for you? I was falling into your arms for warmth when I realised that heaven was in my mind. I fell in love with you, God and myself all at once.

Mirrors

I was indentured in a room profuse of mirrors, drawn to your reflection, an illusion of us feeling like a flower that commences to bloom, like a photograph when times were good, not knowing that the mirror was a mirage tainted with fog. I did not want to leave this room of apparition, shining as though some fantasy of all of my dreams, yearning and skirting my sanity in quaint peculiarity. Let us forget about the sun since he's forgotten us by now. Oh, I wish I could lock myself in this room and lie with you on this floor, and you could kiss me so these sorrows would not turn into strangers. I miss your reflection, like a domicile away from me, a road burden-free chasing highs and lows oh take me home to you. I ponder over the futility of coming here, where there is nothing to look forward to, except a world filled with illusions, unable to comprehend who to trust. But the feeling of your lips leaves me wanting for more, akin to a dry mouth with a conscience. While I cannot leave this room, there is no use looking out, for it is within that brings the solitary feeling, of being alone again, of loneliness. So I will perpetuate prehending and holding on tightly to this mirror when the reflection feels good. Because to me, good times are only those when I remain immersed in your thoughts, my love.

Don't ever let go,

(You have to let go).

I can't let go,

(It is time to let go).

Even the *Darkness*

Has Arms

My heart was battering, so tangled and twined in your skin, bounded by the zealousness in your eyes and your flame was guzzling my shadows. One night of magic rush, the start was a simple touch, and as you ineluctably pulled me off my bed, you made me dance to the songs in my head. I was blinded by the hankering of your love as our intimacy alimented towards the night. O love, you came to me like a dream in this endless night and we lay hand in hand while the world turned egregious. We were just two flames, blazing in your fireplace and you murmured to me your secrets, and I assured you "Do not fear". You smiled at me and I felt your breath as it brushed my cheeks, you kissed the scars in my heart. In a veil full of surprise was a howling beast that could hear us talk through the thin walls. How I only wish I knew about the beast inside of you! Consumed by your pretentious love, ignoring all the big warning signs, I was an imprudent fragile spine, astray in the darkness. I thought I had stumbled upon my angel. Despite the comprehension of your absence, I can feel your lips.

I am afraid I have become a slave to my own heart.

Don't ever let go,

(You have to let go).

I can't let go,

(It is time to let go).

The Ranch Rabbit's

Farmhouse

With my rattled bones on a tardy night, I was running around endeavouring to find our love underground. My reverence for you proved to be akin to boundless and abysmal riches that night as on the west side of the village was a little farm. Down in the farm the shadow grew, but in light of cavalry was a farmhouse that lay archaic and unbroken. Concernedly, as I was searching for you, I got a glimpse of hungry wolves howling in the darkness of the night. In fear, I entered the farmhouse for shelter and through the window, I kept searching for you. I saw a resplendent rabbit in the ranch that was keeping it all in a place, just like the thought of holding onto you felt like bulwarking me from my own pain. The unkind darkness did not bring in the moonlight, how was I going to find you? I reckoned you had led me to the house, for you wanted me to remain safe. The crops below could never understand it all, just as the world at large never understood my love for you. Instantly as the sun arose, I escaped from the farm, joyless that I was without you by my side. It was a comely farmhouse that forfended me, and you were like the farmer that protected me from the wolves. But I am afraid, it felt like a house with no home.

Don't ever let go,

(You have to let go).

I can't let go,

(It is time to let go).

The Great *Drive By*

I was wearing your remains and it was slowly eroding my sense of pride. The tardy night breeze was tearing apart the street into two as I was driving back home, driving as expeditiously as I could. Away from the veracity, away from reality, away from a future that I probably feared. I was at a crossroads, crossroads in my own life. I still recollect how you felt, during that magical car ride, when we looked at the street colours. They had then appeared wild, wondrous and veridical. But on this dim moonless night, as I drive past that same street which was once lit and shining, as refulgent as you, my car commenced decelerating. I saw big vehicles in front of me, the lights had started flicking. I took my hands off the controls and I realised it wasn't traffic but fear in the way. Rain came pouring in suddenness, tapping the car window and my face. With a cigarette in my hand, leaning up against a muscle car, I smoked as I thought to myself "My eyes have always tried seeing more than my mind could contemplate." My thoughts kept me awake that night, I decided to move forward as I was driving with wolves' teeth.

Don't ever let go,

(You have to let go).

I can't let go,

(It is time to let go).

A Song For The Dead

The tomb floors were cleaving, the sun was going down. As I despairingly watched you die, I wanted to hear your voice one last time but you wouldn't make a sound. I held you so close to my heart, it felt like you were a part of my skin. The space in my chest remembered your face and as I was relinquishing you, I was mapping your palm. This road, like all others, led to its cessation. I could hear the angels whispering, and the sound sent quivers down my back. They told me to sing a song for you, like Orpheus of Thrace did for the beautiful Eurydice, so I could join you in death. Hence I closed my eyes and began a song "Even if heaven and hell both decide that they are slaked, I resolve to follow you into the dark, into the visually impairing light. Don't go, please don't go, for you're half of me now. " I sang, my tears flowing unrelentingly. As I crooned the song of the dead I could hardly breathe and found myself down in the grave, locked in my head so querulous and impatient, asleep on my deathbed. For a moment people will ambulate over my grave, and I will lay and dream the weather away. I cannot wait to die so I can see you again. You are my heaven.

Don't ever let go,

(You have to let go).

I can't let go,

(It is time to let go).

The Journey

To Lanka

My love for you knows no bounds like Rama's love for Sita. In the hushness of the night, beneath the starlit sky, my warrior heart was hefty as I was drowning in the tears that filled my eyes. In the dense forests of Panchavati, where the ancient trees whispered tales of love and loss, I was much like Sri Rama, who roamed with blemished hope and a bruised heart in the absence of his beloved Sita. Each step I took reverberated the ache within, a yearning that seemed to stretch beyond the bounds of time itself. Once radiant with the light of devotion, my eyes now mirrored the shadows of despair that clouded my soul. Even the mighty Hanuman, ever vigilant in his service, watched with a heavy heart as I stumbled in the prehension of longing as my mind was a prison. The rustle of leaves in the breeze seemed to whisper your name, while the distant call of birdsongs echoed the melody of your voice. The weight of the world felt heartless and I was lost in the memory of your gentle touch. Oh Sita, my beloved Sita, my heart beats for you and despite the depths of despair, I promise to set you free. There is no obstacle or obstruction too daunting, no trial too astringent as I am willing to cross oceans of sorrow, only to wipe away your tears. In the darkness of Lanka, your light still shines, guiding me towards you. I will traverse the ends of the earth and beyond to be reunited with you once more for I cannot withstand this pain anymore. Oh Lakshmana, I feel powerless.

Don't ever let go,

(You have to let go).

I can't let go,

(It is time to let go).

 *Auction*

That determinative day, it felt like death prehended and clutched me so quiet it did not even make a sound. Was I some muse you utilised for mere fleeting joy? I was torn from the inside but the little whispers in the room told me to not give up. I was in an auction, bidding for your love, bidding for us, in the hopes of victoriously triumphing you over. Little did I know there were many bidding for your love. I was still calling for you when I lost sight but Alas! I lost everything when I lost the bid, 'cause I lost you. It felt like the world had crumbled, for my world has always been you. My heart was seized by a sunken numbness, hollow and deserted. My head was filled with thoughts of you, the pieces of feelings of you I had silently nurtured but never expressed. You left me with a lingering soul, and you had turned our love from gold to dust. I grappled to hold the weight of my crumbling soul while letting go, I was emphatically plummeting into my own illusion. Turns out it might be more facile to love you through the eyes of a stranger. I left the auction room with a broken heart. And as I lauded the bidder who won you as the prize, I took one last look at you . As a teardrop rolled from my eye, I looked away and thought to myself "You might be sold, but our story will grow old."

Don't ever let go,

(You have to let go).

I can't let go,

(It is time to let go).

The Blue *Butterfly*

I was a colourless butterfly waiting to be freed, and each time the wind passed by, he whispered scorn, mocking me for everything I lacked. He laughed and scouted me for the colour that the world couldn't see, for all the hues unseen. I was looking around for someone to repaint my wings and defeatingly searching for a touch to bring me to life. Suddenly, in a world where darkness reigned, devoid of strife, you brought colour into my colourless life. Oh, you came like an emancipator, with hues so divine. My saviour! you bathed my world in blue like the vast sky and made this heart of mine shine. I was disoriented in the silence of my own despair, until you whispered words that filled the air with promises of love that seemed so genuine. I was lost in the emptiness until your love set me free; you filled my world with wonder and brought serenity. But like a fleeting dream, they defunced too soon. You suddenly departed and left my colours to wane, leaving me adrift in a monochrome refrain. In the twilight of love, where shadows reside, I thought I'd seek a new dawn where colours abide. Though my palette may dim and the world is beginning to turn grey, I'll look out for you, in the rainbows, in the light of a new day. I told myself that even in darkness, the hope that you may return will take flight, and I, the colourless butterfly, would find my respite. But alas! as my wings began to fade, my hope still remained unscathed; in the cruel dance of time, I fear I am dying, and my dreams are betrayed. I am now a butterfly of memories, trapped in the past, fading like whispers, too fragile to last. I will now take a promise of a new birth, as my spirit flies, soaring beyond the earth.

Don't ever let go,

(You have to let go).

I can't let go,

(It is time to let go).

 *Bus*

Oh, I took the night bus home, riding through the city's lonely sprawl. There were raindrops on the window and echoed tears, ones that I couldn't show. There were raindrops on the window, nay they were my tears, tears that I wanted to hide from the world. As I looked outside the window, gazing at the empyrean sky, gazing at what could be, I knew not where I was heading. The bus crawled haltingly, every streetlight passing by just accelerating my pain. My thoughts were like tangled webs as I kept in the dark. My memories of us together were like ghosts, haunting every cessation and mark. In the muteness of the night, beneath the city's darkened, masked-up glow, with a heart weighed down by the weight of illusions and erroneous hope, I was disoriented. The bus was taking too long to reach, the driver was lost, I was lost, and our love which had lost its way was peeking through its way in the shadows of the rain . Time was stretched out afore me, like the road that vanished and I was fading into my fears. There was commotion in the bus, and after the driver conclusively navigated his way through, the passengers got off piecemeal. I was the last one to get off. The bus found its way but I could never find my way to you.

I am still lost.

Don't ever let go,

(You have to let go).

I can't let go,

(It is time to let go).

The Shark And

The Fish

Down in the deep depths of love's salty turbulent sea, amidst the whispering currents of ardency, rejection and longing, there subsisted a melancholic dance between an innocuous predator and a profoundly relished prey. I was a loving shark, my sleek form gliding gradually through the water, but my eyes were filled with nothing but admiration and commiseration. And yet, despite my benevolent nature, I found myself drawn to you, a pulchritudinous fish, your scales shimmering like precious jewels in the sunlight. You were so resplendent and ethereal, embodying everything that I dreamt and longed for but could never possess. With each passing day, I watched you from afar, my heart cumbersomely hefty with the weight of unrequited love. I yearned to swim alongside you, to bask in the warmth of your presence, but I knew that such a company could never be. Despite the circumstances I perpetuated to circle around you, offering silent gestures of affection and understanding. I longed to forfend you from the perils of the deep, to shield you from being hurt from the outside world and forfend you from the wild demons of the sea. But alas! you remained elusive, out of reach, a bittersweet reminder of the love that I could never have. Though we may never be together, my mute love for you will endure, a beacon of light for you in the most tenebrous depths of the sea.

Don't ever let go,

(You have to let go).

I can't let go,

(It is time to let go).

The Beggar

I was like a beggar searching for a place to call my own, when I stumbled upon a temple. Its ancient stones were carved with the wisdom of ages weathered by time and standing strong, a saviour from the world's chaos. Within those spiritual halls, I found acceptance, a refuge for my hungry flesh, weary soul. You were a deity enshrined within, my beacon of hope, a guiding light in the darkness of uncertainty. In your embrace, I found my peace. But as I knelt before your altar, basking in your divine presence, whispers began to stir among the temple's devotees. They cast their judgmental gazes upon me, labelling me as a beggar unfit for your love, undeserving of this holy ground. Their words stung like arrows, piercing through the armour of my newfound sanctuary. Yet, despite their judgement, I refused to abandon you, my newfound home. For in you, the god of the temple, I had found a love that transcended the limitations of mortal understanding. It mattered not that I was deemed unworthy by those around me; in the eyes of my deity, I was cherished, valued, and adored. But as the world's clamour grew louder, threatening to tear me away from my sacred haven, I clung to you, my temple god with all the fervour of a devoted disciple. In your presence, I found a sense of belonging I had long sought but never found. Though the world may try to cast me out, I will remain steadfast in my devotion to you, my love unwavering even in the face of adversity. For within the temple's walls, I have found my true home, and I will guard you with all the strength of my heart and soul.

For in your love, I am reborn.

Don't ever let go,

(You have to let go).

I can't let go,

(It is time to let go).

The 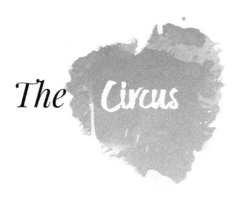 Circus

In the dream of lightness, I was just a clown with painted tears, nebulous and blurring underneath the big top. I was a tightrope walker with some rehearsed routines and tricks that I had learned my whole life. My freedom was bound up, and the weight of prospects was dimming my soul. I knew there was far more than meets the eye until one day your eyes met mine and I felt more free than I had ever been. You were in the audience and as you watched me bring cachinnation into the carnival, juggling, then swinging and leaping from one end to another, I was withal taking a leap of faith. In that brief moment, my love for you gave me the potency and when I conclusively did, you got up and left. When I closed my eyes for just a second, I watched you slip away. In the echoes of applause, I could feel the space and my heartache, through the echoes of laughter was a silent woeful scream. Our love was a haunting echo in this circus of heartbreak. I guess I was just a wandering fool, a regalement and merely a performer to you.

Don't ever let go,

(You have to let go).

I can't let go,

(It is time to let go).

The Withering

Oh fading flower, ! Once so vivacious and profuse of life, she is now ageing and senescent, reaching for the skies, for the firmament. Fighting against despair she is waiting unremittingly to be only revered, but alas! The wind whooshes unsympathetically, knocking her down. Yet she rises and dances with gracefulness unequalled, her fragrance unceasing, bringing smiles to millions. Bathing in sunlight, kissed by the rain, her aeonian patience to be loved and chosen by a honey bee had made her wearisome. She had endeavoured to make herself seen through a field of green but lamentably it was overgrown. Woe! She is withering away, her petals are wallowing, turning to mush. But do the honey bees still not see her agony? Her colours are whispering goodbye and fading to grey. Oh pulchritudinous flower! She is now bowing to the earth, surrendering herself to the journey of the unknown. She waited in hope to be chosen by a honey bee, but only in vain. It fractured her will to live and she, who brought smiles to faces is now dead and gone

Don't ever let go,

(You have to let go).

I can't let go,

(It is time to let go).

The Sinking

I was stranded alone, on a lonely obscure island, far-flung, away from what I once thought was home. There was a void that only silence could fill. I could hear the distance in the quiet, the free welkin made a dreamer like me muse on why some dreams can never be fulfilled. I was probing for my love on that island, one that I might be doomed never to find, yet I searched. You were now a god in my eyes, far above the clouds and the skies, I was holding my head high up, looking for light. I was deserted. Dusk broke in, like you broke my tender heart. I was hungry and left Pat Malone. A part of me intuited I would before long shuffle off this mortal body, yet a part of me would never give up. My love for you was what kept me holding out until night sentineling my hope in life, for the tenebrosity, she will come and I had nowhere left to run but I am trepidacious it was too tardy. I went to look for a safe place for slumber that night, safe from the wilderness. Thenceforward when retraced to that same spot, a voice from my head propounded the truth of how I was whirlpooled in empty circles. The island was submerging, just like my heart was sinking. Yet I still kept standing by in anticipation, in false hopes I gave myself, days before I died a disappearing death.

Don't ever let go,

(You have to let go).

I can't let go,

(It is time to let go).

The Hidden

I sought deliverance, an escape from life on that tardy night when I was expeditiously pacing, endeavouring to find a new world underground when suddenly I was drawn to the haze of cigarettes and bourbon. I stumbled across hidden bars and speakeasies, and in one of them, amidst the crackle of old vinyl and the scent of aged wine, I found you. In the blur of lights, we met again that fateful night, as I watched you guzzle your whiskey. Oh, your heavenly eyes were like a symphony, drawing me closer to you. Instantaneously I fell in love all over again, so much that I wanted to blow the roof off this town. Who knew I'd be falling in love in a bar so cold? We danced together as the echoes of the past became our love song. As the whiskey was burning and stories unfolding, the last song and the night grew cold. I prehended memories that both hearts did still hold and while we danced, I could smell the scent of aged wood and whiskey on your breath. I looked into your eyes, knowing it was the most happy I had ever been. I looked into your eyes, knowing it to be the happiest moment I had ever known. The lights suddenly went off. I could not find you. The fear, the consuming trepidation of losing you again made things so dubious. For a moment there appeared a ray of hope, a light in the window passed through and illuminated the bar, but you were nowhere to be found. I had lost you, again.

I tried to find solace in life's bittersweet depth, but I failed. Again.

Don't ever let go,

(You have to let go).

I can't let go,

(It is time to let go).

The Hamster *Wheel*

Your gleaming eyes, sweet smile, and divine presence was a beguiling spinning wheel, and I was just a hamster in a cage, running in circles with all my thoughts, trapped in fear and unfathomable pain. In the relentless cycle of longing and heartache, I was endlessly chasing after a love that always seemed just out of reach. I was off with a shot at the start, but my legs had begun to tremble from the strain. Round and round the wheel spun on, but I could not find the love that came across as gone. I now find myself caught in a never-ending loop of despondency and disillusionment. No matter how fast I run, I can never seem to bridge the gap between where I am and where I long to be. I miss the life I left behind. And yet, despite the futility of it all, it now dawns upon me that I cannot stop. Your mere existence propels me forward, driving me to run faster and faster, even as my legs give away and my heart grows heavier with each passing moment. I am unable to break free from the boundless grip of my love for you. But amid all this chaos, I can see a glimmer of hope. Perhaps, if I can summon the tenacity to step off the wheel to break free from the cycle, I might decamp. And who knows ! I could at last find the love I have been searching for all along. Deep within my heart I know I will stay trapped in this cycle with no escape. I will endlessly keep running till I get embraced.

I know I will soon be a dead hamster

Don't ever let go,

(You have to let go).

I can't let go,

It is time to let go).

Unopened Doors

You were at my doorstep that night while the moon was hanging low. And as the doorbell kept ringing just like your absence rang in my ears, I sat there in timidity. That night, I went into a deep slumber plagued by another ghost inside of me, with shadows filling the room and all my sorrows coming to drown. My heart was like a sinking balloon and the thought of you made another one sink to the floor. That night, despite my broken home and my weary bones, if I opened the door and the stars and the sky were all mine, I would have willingly given them all to you. I would have plucked it down right from the empyrean sky and left it only ebony. I was never fazed by the darkness in your soul and if on that dark night, had I opened the door and the stars were mine, I would have put them in a jar and given them to you. You stood on the other side in pain, pounding to hear my voice but not half as much as I was aching to hear yours. You tried to find your way back home to me, like a gambler who endeavoured to win back what was lost, hoping that ache would go but I did not open the door. Well, sometimes I wish I did. I could stay locked up in this fantasy, forever. I always wish I did.

Don't ever let go,

(You have to let go).

I can't let go,

(It is time to let go).

The Cattle *Farm*

In the kind breeze of the sprawling fields, I was a goat who found her home in the warmth of a welcoming farm, a sanctuary from the harsh world of yonder. The tender touch of the sun upon my back and the tempting whispers of the wind in the meadows lulled me into a sense of security I had never known. In the gentle eyes of you, my owner, I found a kindred spirit, a friend in a world of strangers. A place where I belonged, no longer alone. You welcomed me with open arms, I felt so free! But little did I know of your fiendish motives. Oh, how I had revelled in the care and affection you had lavished upon me, nurtured with love and trust that knew no bounds. Each day, as I grazed upon the lush green pastures, I felt gratitude bloom within me, for I had found a saviour in you. Then came that fateful day when the truth was laid bare, shattering the fragile illusion of safety I had so fervently clung to. In the cold embrace of the abattoir, I stood face to face with my destiny, a sacrificial lamb led to the slaughter. Your betrayal cut deep, a wound that pierced the very core of my being, yet amidst the pain and anguish, a flicker of understanding blossomed within me. For in the eyes of you, my owner, I saw not malice, but desperation, a hunger born of necessity that drove you to sacrifice my life for your own survival. And though the blade fell swift and true, bleeding and in pain, I could not bring myself to harbour resentment or hatred. For love, I realised, is a force more powerful than pain or betrayal, a bond that transcends even the darkest depths of despair. And so, as I took my final breath, I offered forgiveness to you, my owner, my lord.

For despite your act of betrayal, I found redemption, and in your love, I found peace.

Don't ever let go,

(You have to let go).

I can't let go,

(It is time to let go).

# Old *And Grey*

I keep holding up your end of the bargain as I wait each day for you to return. Every evening, as the sun's fiery kiss bids farewell to the day, I sit by the window, gazing into the distance, waiting for your footsteps, yearning for the sound of the door creaking open and the warmth of your embrace enveloping me. Our empty home echoes with your name. As I recount the little joys of our children growing up, their laughter and innocence that you never saw, became a temporary balm to my pain. In this letter, I share with you the intricate details of our days, the mundane yet beautiful moments that made up our lives together, hoping to bridge the chasm between us with my words. Through this letter, as I relive those beautiful moments of our togetherness, I hope to bridge the gorge between us. Our faithful dog, who you bound with joy with your voice full of love now lies still in death, his once healing presence now a reminder of your painful absence. That faithful friend, now away from sight, left a void splitting my heart with a knife. But still, I wait, holding onto the hope that someday you will return, that someday you will choose me again. I know not why you left. I wonder what stops you from returning back. But I know our bond is so strong, it could withstand the trials of distance and time. I continue to write, I continue to pour my heart onto these pages, hoping that somewhere, somehow, my words will reach you and bring you back to me forever. Yet I fear that you may never return, that our love may never find its way back to where it once belonged. But I shall keep writing these letters, come what may, holding onto the little I have left of you. It is hard to keep alive the hope that you would come back some day. For I fear your memory would fade, old and grey and empty that I am now.

Nevertheless, I shall never stop writing to you till the day we meet in heaven

Don't ever let go,

(You have to let go).

I can't let go,

(It is time to let go)

Wax Wings

I was much like Icarus soaring on wings of wax and dreams, my driving force being my love for you. With each beat of my heart, I ascended ever higher, drawn inexorably towards you much like the Helios' glow, the effulgent sun that blazed on the horizon, a beacon of hope in the vast expanse of the sky. My wings, crafted with care and fuelled by passion, carried me ever closer to you, my beloved. Your warmth was a testament to the fire that burned within my soul. With each burning kiss of Apollo's rays, I flew stoutheartedly, casting aside all doubts and fears, my gaze fixed unwaveringly on the distant glow that beckoned me forward. But as I drew near, the sun's fervent heat began to take its toll, melting the delicate wax that bound my wings together. With each passing moment, the fabric of my dreams began to unravel, wisps of smoke trailing behind me as I struggled to maintain my course. In a moment of heartbreaking clarity, I realised the folly of my pursuit, the futility of chasing after a love that could never be mine. With a heavy heart and wings heavy with sorrow, I watched you slip from my grasp, the sun fading into the distance. And then, with a final, desperate cry, I plummeted from the heavens, my wings crumbling to dust as I fell. In that fleeting moment of freedom, I tasted the bittersweet ecstasy of your love's embrace, only to have it torn away from me in the blink of an eye. As I tumbled towards the earth below, I knew that my journey had reached its end; my dreams shattered like so many shards of glass scattered upon the wind. But even as I fell, I found solace in knowing that my love for you would endure for however long I might survive. My wings are decayed and I will die soon, my love. Truth is, though my wings will crumble, my love remains, a testament to the passion that forever reigns, even in my death.

Don't ever let go,

(You have to let go).

I can't let go,

(It is time to let go).

Printed in the USA
CPSIA information can be obtained
at www.ICGtesting.com
CBHW062029220624
10508CB00021B/1235

9 789362 617224